The Hornets in My Stomach

JAMIE WYMAN

The Hornets in My Stomach Copyright © 2017 Jamie Wyman
Instagram: @headswillr0ll

No part of this book may be used or reproduced in any manner whatsoever without written permission from the author except in the case of brief quotations embodied in critical articles and reviews.

Cover art and internal art by Koda
Instagram: @artofkoda

All rights reserved.

ISBN: 1975811682
ISBN-13: 978-1975811686

To anyone who has been hurt by love, struggled with mental illness, or been stung by hornets – this is for you.

To anyone who has been in love, found recovery, or been kissed by a sunflower – this is for you.

CONTENTS

Hornets   Pg. 1

Hurting   Pg. 27

Hearts   Pg. 47

Healing   Pg. 73

Home   Pg. 93

Hornets

THE HORNETS IN MY STOMACH

When Love is Fear

My heart beats so loudly when you kiss me, you can probably hear it. I hope to god you don't hear it. I don't want you to know how scared you make me. My hands tremble as I hold yours; my knees shake as you spread them open.

You are sleeping next to me in bed, but it feels like a loaded gun is laying down beside me. You have the ability to destroy me any second, but I still trust you enough to fall asleep next to you with your hand on the trigger.

I've always heard of love described as butterflies in your stomach. There are no butterflies. Instead, there are hornets buzzing furiously inside my stomach. Love with you isn't fluttery excitement – it's stinging, stabbing pain.

When I was a child, I was deathly afraid of the monster under my bed. I grew out of that fear, until I met you. I know that there were never any monsters under my bed, but now I lay in fear of the monster beside me in bed.

I learned before that wolves tend to hunt vulnerable prey, like weak or sick deer, since strong and fit animals can easily defend themselves. I've realized that maybe this is why you chose me to love. I was easy to kill and devour.

Sometimes
I can still feel your hard lips
pushing up hard against mine
and filling my throat
with your smoky breath.

Sometimes
I can still feel your rough hands
scratching my soft skin and
rushing to touch where
they shouldn't.

It feels wrong.
It felt wrong.
I don't know why
I let it happen.

THE HORNETS IN MY STOMACH

I let you touch me
where you shouldn't
and taste all the
hidden parts of me,
thinking that if
you fuck me,
you might begin
to love me.

You took me, and I let you.
I stared up at the ceiling
while your hands roamed
and touched where they
wanted to while ripping
off my clothes.

Your teeth bit through my
skin like a wolf's, and your
claws ravaged me as if I
were a struggling fawn.

I felt like I wasn't there,
like I wasn't me, and
I could feel my soul
dripping down through
the mattress.

I cried on the walk home,
not because you had touched
me where you shouldn't have,
but because I had left myself
within your mattress.
I left something there
that I will never get back.

I am not me anymore.

THE HORNETS IN MY STOMACH

Dissociation

He is on top of me.
I can feel myself
s e p a r a t i n g
discon | necting
and I am looking
down on us
from the ceiling
as he splits me
in half, right
between my legs.

Things I Wish I Would've Known Before I Met You

1. I think I mistook the hornets in my
stomach for butterflies. Your kisses made
me numb to the paralyzing stings in the
pit of my gut.

2. My hands shook and my knees quivered
and I couldn't breathe. I should've known
that this was fear, not excitement. This was
pain, not pleasure. This was death, not love.

3. I didn't know it at the time but, sleeping
with you wasn't going to ease the pain from
my broken heart. It would only stomp on the
remaining pieces left shattered on the ground.

4. I was not me when I met you. I wish I
would've known that after meeting you,
I would never be me again. You took me
away from myself.

5. The guilt from letting you take me would
stay with me longer than the hickeys you
left upon my neck and thighs. I still have
not been able to wash it off.

THE HORNETS IN MY STOMACH

i. He is made of shadows, but I am so engulfed in blackness that even he looks like he's made of light. I've lived so long in darkness that I long for any type of warmth, even if it's just from a few minutes of his body on top of mine.

ii. He never stays. He leaves my body more broken than it was when he first touched it. By the time I notice the empty space beside me in bed, he is already gone. Can't you stay, just one time? Can't you love me, just once?

iii. I tear apart the house looking for any trace of him. I rip open my chest to hopefully find some fragment of him inside of my ribcage. I know he doesn't love me, but maybe he left something in my heart.

iv. Is it still a one-night stand if it happens every night? Why does he only love me when he takes my clothes off? Am I a poor excuse for a lover? Love is supposed to be soft, but why does his love feel so painful? Why does it hurt?

I had severe depression when I met you
and I remember I felt really numb.
I think the reason why I let you
touch me and have your way with me
was because I could finally feel something.
It was a terrible feeling, not the usual
pitter-patter of my heart, but more like
each heart beat screaming like a gunshot.
You gave me the worst feeling in my
chest, but at least I could finally feel.
I hadn't felt anything in so long,
but for the first time, I felt something,
even though it was a bad something.
But now I realize that you made me
feel too much. Ever since I met you,
I've had bullets in my chest and
hurricanes in my head and I want to
stop feeling again.

THE HORNETS IN MY STOMACH

I've let people touch me that didn't deserve it.
I've let people have me that didn't treat me
like a human being. I regret it so damn much.
I can't un-touch myself. I can't take off their
fingerprints no matter how hard I scrape my
skin in the shower night after night after night.
I was ruined and I do not know how to build
back my walls. They always say that your
body is a temple, but they never give you
blueprints on how to rebuild it after it gets
torn down. They always say that your body
is a temple, but I do not know how to treat
it as such. I treat it like a shitty motel where
men come and go like flighty travelers that
do not want to stay. How do I make my body
sacred? How do I remove the cockroaches
and the cum-stained bedsheets and the peeling
wallpaper? How do I build up my walls
into a golden temple?

I met the devil when I was twelve.
He spun a bottle and took me in a
closet to show me what seven
minutes in heaven looked like.

My mother told me that heaven was filled
with golden sunlight and warm clouds
and angels who sing and kiss you gently.

Heaven was a dark closet and a cold floor
and hard kisses and sharp fingernails in my
skin and heavy arms holding me down.
I did not find grace in that heaven behind
closed doors, but rather regret and contrition.

The devil does not have horns or fangs or
a tail pointed like an arrow. The devil is
every boy who takes girls against their will
in closets, in bedrooms, in alleyways, in cars.
The devil is every boy who sucks the soul
out of girls who crumble apart within his fists.
The devil is every boy who uses girls to sin
without ever begging for forgiveness.

THE HORNETS IN MY STOMACH

My skin still remembers your touch.
I wake up screaming at night with
bleeding scratches on my thighs
because I had tried to claw your
fingers out from my body.
I don't know how to forget your
touch without cutting it out of my
flesh. It hurt when you touched me
and it hurts to get rid of you.
I can still feel my skin crawl when
it remembers how your rough
hands felt. My skin can't forget
you and my heart can't forgive you.
How do you forget a touch when it
put you together but ripped you
apart at the same time?

I don't know why I still wear your sweater.
Maybe it's because I still crave your touch
in some weird and twisted way, even though
you had always touched too much.
Maybe it's because the sweater gives me
the warmth that you never gave me.
Maybe it's because I still like to think of you,
even though it makes my stomach feel sick.
I don't know why I still wear your sweater.
Maybe it's because it stayed when you left.

THE HORNETS IN MY STOMACH

What You Left Behind

1. You left two of your sweaters with me.
The first: I said I would bring it back,
but I forgot. The second: I got out of your
car but never saw you again to return it.

2. You left your old texts on my phone.
Rather, you sent them and I didn't have
the guts to delete them.

3. You left bite marks and hickeys on my
skin. They have faded since then, but I
haven't forgotten about them and how
you placed them on me.

4. You left regret inside my heart.
Out of everything you left behind,
regret is the one that hurts the most.

5. You left behind me. I don't feel lost,
I don't feel forgotten. I feel ignored,
abandoned, tossed away. I guess that
shouldn't surprise me. I knew that I
meant nothing to you in the way you
kissed me with no fire in your throat.

I am thinking of you tonight
and it scares me so much
that I cannot fall asleep.

I can almost feel your
tongue down my throat again
and I think I'm choking.

I can almost feel your
teeth on my thigh again
and I think I'm bleeding.

I can almost feel your
fingers inside me again
and I think I'm dying.

You crawled your way into
my chest from between my
legs and now you won't leave.

I am trying to push you out,
but you had your way with me
and now you won't let me go.

A wolf never lets go of a
kill once it has the neck
clamped between its jaws.

All I was to you was prey.
All I was to you was a deer to
kill and devour for pleasure.

THE HORNETS IN MY STOMACH

You haven't thought about him in months,
and you're really proud of that, considering
you couldn't get him out from underneath
your skin for a year. You finally stopped
writing painful poems about him. You blocked
him on every social media site you have,
but one day, his name pops up on your screen.
"Hey, what's up?"
You tell yourself, "I don't need you or
your apology."
You tell yourself, "I am in love now, with a
boy much better than him. I love a boy who
treats me like gold, when he stomped on me
like I was dirt."
You tell yourself, "I am not dirt."
You tell yourself, "I am much better now."
BLOCK ACCOUNT
"Are you sure you want to block this account?"
You hesitate.
You ask yourself, "Why do I still feel the need
to talk to him, to explain myself?"
You ask yourself, "Why does he upset me so
much? Why does he still control me?
You ask yourself, "What if I am dirt?"
CONFIRM

Regrets Personified

My regrets came to me
wearing a too-large black
t-shirt and messy, dark hair.
He rang my doorbell and
I got into his shitty white
jeep and drove off in the
opposite direction of my
innocence.

I never knew the taste of
shame until it kissed my
lips. I never knew the feel
of guilt until it entered
between my legs. I never
knew the pain of
disappointment until it
bit into my skin.
But now I know.

My regrets left me one
night, even after all the
times I let him take me.
Regret doesn't care if
you give him your heart
or your thighs. Regret
takes and takes and
never gives you back.

THE HORNETS IN MY STOMACH

Advice I Wish that I had Heard Before Him

If your fingers tremble on the hooks of your bra,
trying to unhook it, do not make love to that boy.
If looking at his eyes make you feel like you are staring
into the eyes of a ghost, do not make love to that boy.
If his hands scratch your skin and rush to touch places
that are not your heart, do not make love to that boy.
If you feel like there are stones stuck in your throat while you
watch him unbutton his jeans, do not make love to that boy.
If your stomach feels like hornets stinging you while
he is roughly kissing you, do not make love to that boy.
Do not make love to boys who make you feel afraid.

I carry so much guilt that it is difficult for me to hold your hand. Guilt is everywhere. It's under my skin and it's in between my teeth and it's in my hair. He gave it to me, but he won't leave, even though he's been gone for years. He lives in the deep recesses of my mind, coming out sometimes when I'm trying to sleep at night, like the rats scratching around the attic at midnight. I know he's gone but he is still here. He is still here when I hold your hand and I feel his rough palms. He is still here when I kiss you and I remember the taste of his alcohol breath. He is still here when you are making love to me and I have flashbacks of the things he did to me. He is still here when I look at you on top of me and I see him instead. I feel guilty. You are nothing like him – you never were, you never will be. But it's not like I see him in you. I feel like I will see him in everyone I will ever try to love.

THE HORNETS IN MY STOMACH

You cannot be a ghost that haunts me for the rest of my life.
I am not an old house that you can reside in and terrorize.
I am not a tombstone in a cemetery that you can dwell in.
I've tried to rid the skeletons from my closets, nail crucifixes
to every wall, place candles upon your grave, and wear rosary
beads around my throat, but you keep coming back to haunt
me. I see manifestations of you everywhere – the car you
used to drive when you picked me up, the black sweater you
used to wear as you undressed me, the remnants of your name
that flashes on my cell phone screen. I see you in the eyes of
my lover and I know I am possessed. I scream religious chants
in my sleep to rid you from my nightmares, but you still
terrorize my dreams every night. I cannot forget you because
you will not forget me. You refuse to let go of the memories
of when we were together and you're taking me into the
afterlife with you. You're dragging me into the ground next
to your grave. I am dying an early death because of you.
You cannot handle me being alive and happy without you,
so you won't let me. What do I do? What do I do when
you've become a ghost that haunts me endlessly?

Parallels

I like the idea of parallel universes.
I can't change what happened, so I
pretend things that could've happened.

In another universe, I said, "no."
I pushed you off of me and yelled
and fought for myself.

In another universe, I was able to
rescue myself from you. I was my
own savior.

In another universe, I didn't go back
to you so many times. I actually didn't
go back to you at all.

In another universe, I loved myself
enough to not let myself get hurt
by you.

In another universe, I didn't blame
myself for what you did to me. I
I could see that it was your fault.

In another universe, I didn't meet
you. We never knew each other.
I didn't even know that you existed.

But in this universe, I met you.
I let you have me over and over. I
blame myself. I can't forgive myself.

THE HORNETS IN MY STOMACH

I repress everything bad in my mind so that I don't
have to think about it. It's like burying dead bodies.
The reek of corpses is clouding my mind and
sometimes, the memories slip out and I cannot breathe.
I do not know how to get over things, so I bury it all instead.
I do not want to feel things, so I push it all away.
I know that I cannot bury things forever. All cemeteries
eventually run out of room for the souls that lie within them.
I can feel my head throbbing because I am trying to fit
too many dead bodies into it.
A person can only hide so many skeletons,
but my mind cannot be a graveyard.

A Letter to Myself

I'm sorry that men have touched you in ways that made you
afraid for any other man to touch you ever again.
I'm sorry that you first learned fear from a hand on your thigh.
I'm sorry that you learned to think of hornets in your gut as
butterflies in your stomach, of fear as excitement, of pain as love.
I'm sorry that you grew up to think of sex as shameful,
disgusting, and painful.
I'm sorry that I let you stay in his arms, even though you were
terrified. I'm sorry that I didn't let you run away.
I'm sorry that a part of your heart is still left inside of his mattress.
I'm sorry that I let you stay for as long as you did.
I'm sorry that the regret from everything
has still not come out from under your skin.
I'm sorry that you still hurt, even years and years later.
I'm sorry that you cannot find safety,
even in the boy you love most.
I'm sorry that you don't feel at home in his arms,
or anyone's arms, because of what happened.
I'm sorry for the flashbacks and I'm sorry for the memories.
I'm sorry for the overwhelming pain that
still hurts your heart after all this time.
I'm sorry for repressing your emotions for so long.
I'm trying so hard to forgive myself for letting everything happen,
but it's so damn hard. This is my apology to you.
Please learn to forgive me.

Hurting

Things Nobody Tells You About Depression

1. They tell you depression means sadness, but they don't tell you how unbearable that sadness is. They don't tell you how it feels to suffocate under the weight of your own misery. They don't tell you how it feels to be so sad that you'd rather die than feel it anymore.

2. Nobody will really understand you when you tell them about your depression. You will be bombarded with inconsiderate phrases like, "Just get over it," "It's all in your head," and, "Other people have it worse. You're fine."

3. No one ever tells you how to survive depression. No one tells you how to suffer through the pain, how to survive those long, sleepless nights, how to stop crying, how to refuse the urge to cause pain to yourself. No one tells you how to save you from yourself.

4. People will always tell you that you are not alone, but you are always alone. Nobody is ever there when you are crying so hard that it feels like your eyes will fall out of the sockets. Nobody is ever there when you turn to self-harm. Nobody is ever there when you're curled up on the floor of your shower, letting your tears mix in with the cold water falling upon you.

5. Your depression follows you everywhere. It does not go away. It always overshadows you like a heavy morning fog. You won't be able to see or think clearly. You won't be able to feel, or you will feel too much. Every-where you look, it's there. You'll want depression to leave, but it's the only one that's there when you are truly alone.

Living Corpse

I wanted to die, but not this way.
Death is not a beautiful thing,
but the way I'm killing myself is hideous.
I've never imagined my death,
but I always thought that
maybe it would be better than this.
I have already died on the inside
and now my outside is catching up.
I'm planning my funeral before it happens.
I call my mother and tell her that
I've been carving my name into my tombstone.
I try to smile and laugh but
I've already placed flowers on my grave.
I kiss my lover on the lips before
I lower myself into the ground.
I always felt I wouldn't live that long,
but I never thought it would end like this.
This is how it feels to have a heartbeat
and a steady breath but to still be dead.

THE HORNETS IN MY STOMACH

I can't love you when depression gets in the way.
I try so hard to be happy for you,
but I really don't know how.
I know you feel like you are holding me,
but you love me too much to see that
you are holding a lifeless skeleton.
I am only a pile of broken bones.
I have no potential,
no future, nothing.
I am a wasted life that you are
putting too much hope into.
I should've warned you that
falling in love with me is a trap.
I should've told you not to get too attached
to me because I will not stay for long.
I'm sorry I made you fall in love with me
when my very existence is so fleeting.
I cannot guarantee my love and I cannot
guarantee that I will spend my life with you
because I know I might end it someday.
You always tell me to stop saying that
you can find someone better than me,
but you deserve someone who will
stay alive for you.

What does Depression feel like?

i. It feels painful – a constant pain. A pain that doesn't end. It's a pain in the center of my chest, like I got punched and knocked backwards, and I'm left on the ground, gasping for air. Sometimes, the pain is in my heart, and it hurts so much that I want to cut it out of my chest to make it stop. It's a sharp emotional hurt, but it becomes so painful that it turns into physical agony. It makes me want to die so that I won't have to hurt anymore.

ii. It feels like however darkness would feel. If shadow was a feeling, that's how it would feel like. I feel dark all the time. I see no light in anything. Nothing brings me joy or happiness anymore. Darkness is just the absence of light, but it feels so heavy. It sits on my shoulders and I can feel my spine snapping because of its weight. It drags you down, always. You're always being pulled down by this evil, dark shadow that doesn't go away. It doesn't leave you alone.

iii. It feels like drowning. It's like when you are swimming out in the ocean on a day when the waves are strong. You can see the shore, but the more you struggle to swim, the farther away you get from land. It pulls you away from all that keeps you alive and sane. You struggle to stay above water, but you get weak eventually, and it pulls you under. You lose the strength to breathe and you swallow the cold water and die. It kills you. There's no easy way to say it, but it kills you.

Suicide Note – 2:15 am

Death
reaches out to me
with his cold hand
and asks me
to waltz.
I'll take his hand
and dance
my life away.

I am a broken poet
with a broken heart
and a broken life
and a broken love
and a broken soul.
I write wrenching
words on paper to
ease the pain in my
broken mind but
the more I write,
the more I am
reminded of what
made me so broken
in the first place.

I am a broken poet
with a broken brain
and a broken back
and a broken future
and a broken past.
I write when I
cannot sleep at 3am
and my thoughts
pierce my mind
like stabbing knives.
I write when I am
so lonely that it feels
like my heart is
ripping open.

I am a broken poet
with a broken bottle
and a broken home
and a broken will
and a broken spirit.
I write about loves
I've had and loves
I've never had and
mostly, I write about
you, and how you've
taken over my body
like a tree's roots
growing in concrete,
entirely and completely.

THE HORNETS IN MY STOMACH

3 a.m. Thoughts

I hate my life. I really do.
I don't want to live my life.
Most of the time, I feel like
I am only here because others
want me here. I stay because
they would be sad if I left.
They'd have to live through
me being gone forever, and
I couldn't bear to put anyone
through that. But do I want to
live my life for myself? No.

I wish that I didn't have
anyone tying me to this earth,
or I'd leave it. The people
I love are chains that keep me
here when I'd rather leave.
My soul wants to be free, but
it's trapped in this shitty body in
this shitty life in this shitty world.

An Apology Letter

I'm sorry that my mouth is always so
full of Prozac that you can't kiss me.
I'm sorry I'm so dead inside that you
have to constantly revive me, draining
your happiness just so I can breathe
once again.
I'm sorry that I'm never alive and in
the moment. I look at you with empty
eyes that see absolutely nothing.
I'm sorry that you have to give a part
of yourself to me so I can be whole.
I'm sorry that when my sadness
washes over me like a tidal wave, I
grab your hand and make you drown
with me.
I'm sorry my depression has not only
made it difficult for me, but for you, too.

Loving a Girl with Depression

i. I remember the first time she broke down in my arms. I didn't know what to think or do. She always looked like she carried the mountains on her shoulders so effortlessly. But now she crumbled apart under the weight and I was left to support her. I didn't know if I could lift the both of us without our love being crushed as well.

ii. I never know where to touch her without breaking her even more. Where do I put my hands on her if she hurts everywhere? I'm trying so hard to be gentle. I don't want to cause her any more pain than what she's been through. I want to make her stop hurting, but I don't know how.

iii. I am trying to love softly. I love her so much that I want hard kisses and reckless feelings and sex so passionate that the neighbors can hear her moaning my name. But I need to be gentle. I'm willing to give her soft kisses, and I realize that she is more careful with her feelings than I am.

iv. I hate it when she cries. It hurts so much to know that the one I love the most is in pain. I never know what to do when she cries. All I can do is hold her and refuse to let go until her tears are gone. I hope that's enough for her.

v. I want her to be happy.

The Two Types of Depression

1. There are times when you feel nothing. You feel numb. It doesn't matter if something good or bad happens – you don't notice. Your happiness is gone. So are the rest of your emotions, really. You try to hurt yourself so that maybe you can feel once more. You go through life feeling nothing. You can't remember the last time you smiled, or even cried. You are so numb that you wish you could feel something again.

2. There are other times when you feel everything. Every emotion rushes into you at once, and you feel like you got hit by a car. Your heart feels like it fell out from your throat, and you curl up in a ball on the bathroom floor, trying to keep yourself together. Feeling so much and so deeply hurts, and it makes you wish you could go back to feeling nothing at all.

THE HORNETS IN MY STOMACH

Depression as Types of Pain

Chest Pain: This kind makes you feel like your entire being is collapsing in on itself. You clutch your chest as you cry to keep your heart from falling out. This pain is the kind that leaves you crying on the bathroom floor, gasping for air, but feeling like you never want to take another breath. It's the pain that hits you in the pit of the stomach, like you got the wind knocked out of you.

Migraine: This is depression is a sharp stabbing pain. You take too many pain killers to make it go away, but it never does. You can't see this pain, but you know it's there. It's the kind of pain that makes you lay down in bed for hours in the darkness, pounding and throbbing and moaning and groaning. This depression keeps you up at night. Who can sleep with a sadness so aching?

Open Wound: This depression is fresh and new. Maybe it's a breakup. Maybe it's a death. Maybe it's heartbreak or loneliness or regret or longing or hatred or anything else. But it's recent and it hurts. You still remember how it felt to be hurt when it happened. You look at the wound and remember your lover's words, "I can't do this anymore," or your father's words, "You will never be good enough," or your friend's words, "Stop calling me." It stings when you sleep and it stings when you shower and it stings when you put a shirt over it and it stings when you remember what happened and it stings when you try to heal and it stings when you can't forget.

Bruise: This depression is visible. You can see the dark blacks, blues, and purples under your skin. This is depression that wants to be seen. This depression is the kind people notice. They ask, "Are you okay?" and "Are you feeling alright?" But you cover your bruise and say, "I'm fine." You don't want people to know how bad it has gotten. This is depression escaping through your skin.

Back Pain: This pain is when depression weighs on your shoulders. You carry it every single day, and it gets heavier and heavier each moment. It never goes away. You live each day with this boulder on your back. A bone can only carry so much sadness until it breaks. It hurts to move and your muscles are stiff. This depression won't let you go. It confines you in your own body. Everything aches. You've learned to hunch under the weight of your depression. It is possible to live with depression, but it's not possible to be alive with it.

JAMIE WYMAN

They always say that
the apple doesn't fall far from the tree.
You knew from a young age that
your father loved alcohol more than you.
He drank it every day,
but saw you only once a month.
He kissed the lips of his beer bottles
more than he kissed your forehead.

The apple doesn't fall far from the tree;
you used to want to swing from its branches.
You were a child and you wanted your father's
love, but he would get so drunk, so very drunk.
He would yell at you and punch holes in the wall.
He became a monster, and you were scared of him.

The apple doesn't fall far from the tree;
you got an axe and chopped it down.
You cut ties with your father, and it's been
almost 6 years since you've last seen him.
You know he doesn't care.
He doesn't call anymore.

The apple doesn't fall far from the tree,
and you've since burned it down.
You're 21 now,
at the age where people go out drinking.
You're terrified of alcohol.
You refuse to let a drop of it touch your tongue.
You don't want to become like your father.
You are the apple, but you've fallen so far
from the tree that you don't know where you are.

THE HORNETS IN MY STOMACH

I made my mother
cry tonight.
She thinks
I am going to
kill myself.
I am a
horrible
horrible
person.
I never meant to
hurt her.
All I wanted to do
was end my own
hurt.
I wish I could
stop existing
without
hurting
anyone else
in the process.
I wish I could
die
quietly
like how a flower
dies
quietly.
Nobody knows
when a flower
dies.

On Helping Someone with Depression when You Suffer from it, Too

i. You come to me smelling of fear, and your face is a storm cloud with raindrops falling from your cheeks down to your chin. You heart is lodged in your throat and your chest is collapsing. You want me to help you breathe, but I am suffocating, too.

ii. I love you, but I don't think that I can save you.

iii. I can help you find happiness, but it drains me of my own. I wish you knew that in helping you, I am risking my own stability.

iv. I cannot give you recovery because I haven't found it myself. But I can give you late night runs to the gas station to get pints of ice cream. I can give you phone calls every night and then every morning to make sure you're okay. I can give you a hand to wipe away the tears when you are crying because life is too heavy on your shoulders.

v. Know that I am broken, too. You want me to pick up your pieces, but how can I do that without falling apart myself? As I bend over to pick up your pieces, my own fall out of my chest. I want to make you whole, but I'd have to give up parts of me to do that.

THE HORNETS IN MY STOMACH

Sometimes,
death does not
let you
pack your bags
or write a
goodbye note
before it grabs
your hand and
takes you away.

Apologies to my Lover

I'm sorry that I am so sad.
I can feel my mental health deteriorating,
and I know it's ruining myself and our relationship.
I don't expect you to understand [you can't].
I'm sorry that when I'm drowning in my sadness,
I grab your hand and drag you down with me.
I don't mean to, but I guess it's a natural reaction
when you're dying.

I think it's time to let go of your hand.

THE HORNETS IN MY STOMACH

I fell apart in the shower tonight.
I crumbled to the floor as if my
bones shattered inside me all at once.
My tears mixed with the water
and I could no longer tell if I was
crying or drowning. My wet body
collapsed from within and I cried
while feeling my heart implode.
I fell apart until the water got cold
and my skin turned pale.

I turned off the shower and stepped
out. I looked at my naked, shivering
body in the mirror. My hair was
soaked in tears, and tears trailed
down my bare skin. My eyes were
red and swollen. Parts of me were
left down the drain – I could see
parts of me were missing. I looked
at my reflection and I could see
that I was losing myself.

I fell apart in the shower tonight.
Sometimes, it takes falling apart
to realize that you are the only
one capable of putting yourself
back together.

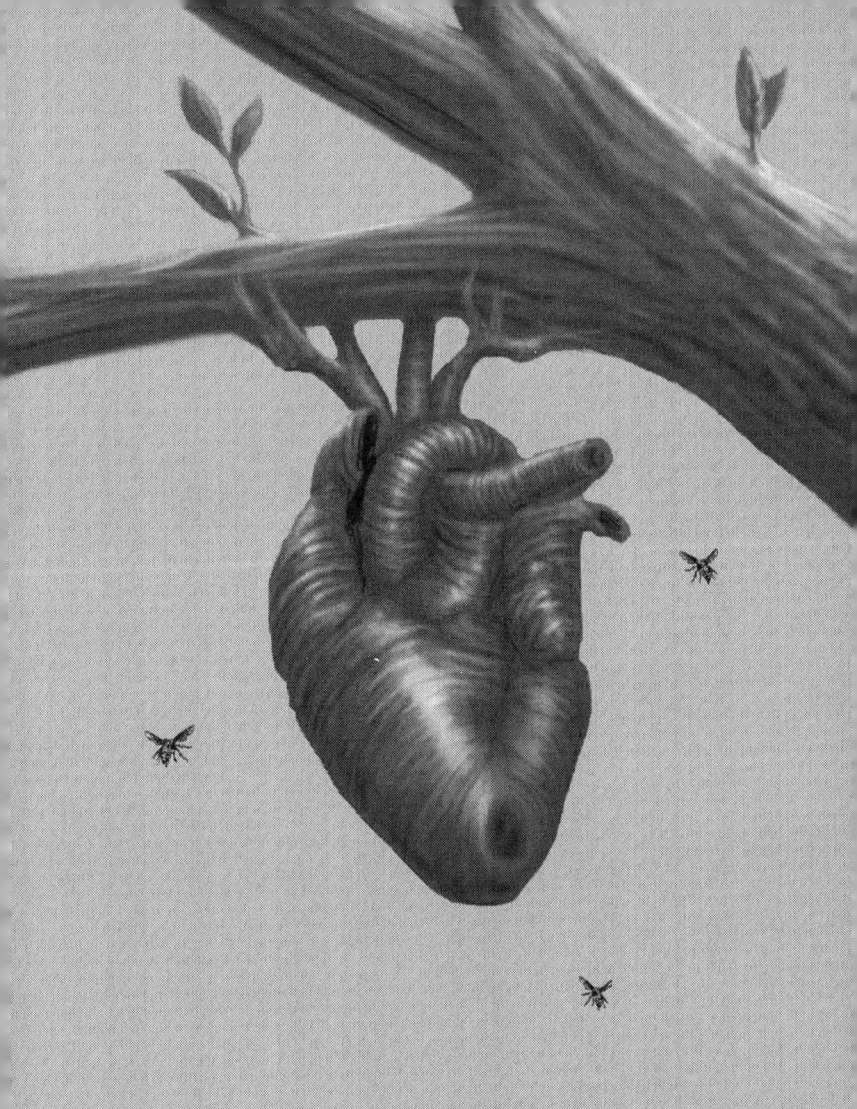

Hearts

THE HORNETS IN MY STOMACH

My heart is a fire hazard.
It has been deprived of love for so long,
that it is a desolate wasteland of dust
and dried up dreams.
Just a single spark of affection
could set me up in flames,
burning me from the inside out.
Don't kiss me if you don't mean it.
Don't tell me you love me if it's a mistake.
Embers falling from your lips could
start an entire forest fire in my chest,
and every limb of me will be destroyed.
I will stand before you,
burning alive,
and I know you wouldn't have the
decency to save me from
the fires you started.

You moved above me like a storm moves across the sky.
Your head blocked out the light of your ceiling fan like
clouds cover up the sun. Your hand reached down to
touch my skin just like lightening comes down to strike
the ground beneath it.

I used to be scared of thunderstorms as a child, but now
I find myself making love to one. I feel every bit afraid
as I did when I was a child, but this time, I can't hide.
I cannot tell the difference between your thunder
crashing and the pounding in my heart.

THE HORNETS IN MY STOMACH

I looked into your eyes and I realized that this
love was much greater than the both of us.
We were entering this world of passionate lust
and pain and sorrow and jealousy and giving
your heart away completely and soft caresses
and longing and missing and kissing and
fingertip touches and holding hands and
broken wrists and broken hearts and broken
love and handwritten letters and flowers
beside the bed and drunken arguments and
living together and having fights and breaking
up and getting back together and regrets and
decisions and forgotten promises and
everything being so perfect yet so flawed.
And maybe that's why we didn't work out.
We were just children playing around with
something we could not yet understand.

You made barbed wire
look like lace.
You made bruises
look like kisses.
You made fear
taste like love.
You took my
broken heart and
made it seem like
it was whole,
even though you
broke it more.
You made me think
that you were an angel,
until I looked up and
saw a devil standing
where you should be.
You showed me fear
with the curl of your lips.
You made sharp things
seem like they were soft,
and I wonder how I could
touch you without bleeding
out too much.

THE HORNETS IN MY STOMACH

I am a ship drifting away from you,
and the lands of your body are
becoming foreign to me.
I had once known each freckled
path on your skin,
but a sailor sometimes forgets
what it is like
to walk on solid ground.

I'm sick of "almost" love,
of relationships full of
broken promises.
"I could've – "
"I would've – "
"I should've – "

But you didn't.

THE HORNETS IN MY STOMACH

How to tell that he's not the one:

1. He gives you a bouquet of sorries,
and though they are lovely, they
wither away within a few days.

2. He writes love notes on your
thighs with hickeys, but he lies
through his teeth with each bite.

3. He has sex with you. It feels
less like making love, and more
like fucking.

4. He puts his tongue in your mouth
and it makes you think how the most
harmful things taste the best.

You told me you needed space
and I thought of
falling into black holes
and burning up in the sun's orbit
and freezing to death on Neptune
and floating in an endless void
and taking off your space
helmet and suffocating.
I think of space and I think of
dying because humans can't
survive there.
You didn't want space,
you wanted to leave me.

But now you're lightyears away
from me and I can feel the
stars in between us. I wonder
how far you will wander
before you realize that you
miss me, or before you
realize that you don't.
I gave you the world,
but you wanted to leave it.
We fell in love in a nebula,
but fell apart in a supernova.

THE HORNETS IN MY STOMACH

Love Shouldn't be a Decision

I wish you knew what you wanted,
and I wish that was me.

I Feel Different

You hold my face
in the palm of your hand,
stroking my cheek
with your thumb.
You stare into my eyes
and you say,
"You look different."
I say that
I do not understand.
You tell me,
"You don't look the same."
I tell you,
"I don't feel the same."
You say that
you do not understand.
I take your hand off my cheek
and I whisper,
"A heart is never the same
after you break it."

THE HORNETS IN MY STOMACH

How to Know He's Fallen Out of Love with You

1. His eyes used to look like the warm, glowing windows of a home you belong in. But the lights have since gone out, and the home has turned into a lonely, abandoned house that no heart has resided in for a long, long time.

2. He used to give you everything – love letters, lockets, flowers, his heart. But now, even his time is too much to ask for, and you don't ask for much. He used to give you everything, but now he gives you nothing.

3. He used to be so warm. He felt like a summer day, and his touch soothed your heart. Somewhere along the way, he became cold towards you. You tried to keep the warmth, but you can't light a fire in a snowstorm.

4. He would always make you his first priority. Lately, you have felt like an annoyance, a burden, a hassle. He makes you feel like you get in the way. He used to treat you like gold, but now you feel like dirt under his fingernails.

5. His love isn't the same anymore. He changed, and his loving kisses have turned into quick embraces. You don't know why this happened, but you do know that nothing will ever be the same again.

I don't think
you know
how terrible
it is to be
laying down
right next
to you
and
still feel
so alone.

Worship

1. You kissed me more than you kissed the cross that hung around your neck. Yet your lips still had a hint of metallic flavor to them.

2. I kissed your lips and tasted a thousand flavors of heaven. I looked into your eyes and saw a thousand visions of hell. Your fingertips touch my soul and I know my heart is trapped in your purgatory.

3. You pinned my wrists to the wall and I felt like Jesus on the cross. Your hands were the nails that pierced through my bones. While your lips were pressed against mine, I wondered if God ever came into your mind as much as you said He did.

4. We made love and you would moan, "Oh God," and that was the closest you'd ever come to a prayer.

5. You read my skin more intently than I ever saw you read your bible. Of the seven deadly sins, lust was the one that killed you.

Let me devastate you.
Let me sink my fangs into your
neck just how you like it.
Let me shatter your bones
from the inside out.
I promise I will make you feel
good if only you let me in.
I will break your heart in the process,
but I swear you'll feel too good
to notice it.
Let me put out the fire burning
in your thighs.
Let me tear apart your skin
so that I can feel every inch of you.
I will complicate you so that you
will no longer know if
you love me or hate me.
Let me ruin you so that
I don't remember how ruined I am.
I can make you love
but I can make you hurt even more.
Let me dominate you.
Let me make you forget him.
Let me make you bad.
You're an angel, but don't you see now
why Lucifer fell from heaven?
Let me kiss you so hard that
you lose your consciousness.
Let my tongue conquer you.
Let my hands pin you down.
Let me do what I want with you.

THE HORNETS IN MY STOMACH

You Can't Control Your Heart

He could hurt you over and over again and you'd still love him because hearts are reckless and charge headfirst into things that kill them.

Inferno

We met and I fell in love with you,
as you did with me. But after a year,
you fell out of love, and I spent that
whole time acting like I didn't know
that this was going to happen.

I know that I don't mean much to
you anymore, but loving you was
like feeling heat from the sunlight
after living in a snowstorm for
years. You brought warmth into
my heart that hadn't been there
in a long time.

I think my problem was that I
loved too hard when you loved
too little. I was a wildfire and
you were the flower that I kissed
with my embers. I burnt you to
ashes when you weren't willing
to warm your hands by my fire.

THE HORNETS IN MY STOMACH

How to Know You've Fallen Out of Love

1. Being in his arms used to feel like he was holding you on top of the world, like you were flying. Now, you're drowning inside of his arms. He became an ocean that crushed you under its waves.

2. Loving him has become habit. Kissing is emotionless. Sex is a chore. You've done all this a million times. It comes natural at this point, but the joy of it is gone. You want something to break the monotony.

3. You look at other people, wondering what it'd be like to be with them instead. Wondering becomes wishing. Wishing becomes longing. Longing becomes needing. Like that, you need to love someone else and get out.

4. Excitement feels like the faint light of a train that has passed, and is now fading off into the distance. You haven't felt butterflies in your stomach for a long time. Maybe they've flown away by now. Maybe they've died.

Fallen Angel

I fell in love with an angel who hid her sins between
the pages of her bible and kissed it shut.
When I first saw her, I nervously stuttered,
"Did it hurt when you fell from heaven?"

I fell in love with an angel who lived in corruption,
who drank red wine like it was the blood of Jesus.
Her halo didn't glow and her wings were broken.
She wasn't pure and she wasn't innocent.

I fell in love with a damned angel who
only said God's name when we made love.
I worshipped her, but even Lucifer was
worshipped before he fell from heaven.

Empty Treasure

I remember reaching into the soil of your chest,
and I kept digging, but all I found was more
dirt where your gold heart should have been.

Two Types of Loneliness

Feeling alone next to the
empty space beside you in bed.
Feeling alone next to the
lover sleeping beside you in bed.

THE HORNETS IN MY STOMACH

If a Heart Breaks in a Forest, but Nobody Hears it, does it Still Hurt?

Maybe it's because I haven't slept
much these past three days,
but I feel like I'm falling apart.
I think you don't love me and it's
splitting my skin like rotting wood.
I am a hollow log, and my heart
feels like it's falling out of
the caverns of my chest.
My trembling hands struggle
to keep my heart inside
of the bloody hole you left.
There is an unbearable emptiness
in my lungs, like you've taken away
my breath with a shaky exhale.
I can't seem to inhale again, no matter
how painfully my chest convulses.
But none of that matters
because you don't love me.
I've fallen apart before, but you
were there to fix me with your lips.
Now you're gone.
You don't care, and I am decaying.
I am a dying tree with our initials
still carved into my flesh.

I've always been a hotel for people. My heart contains rooms for traveling lovers to stay until they decide to leave me. People come and go as they please, but I've never met anyone who has decided to stay. I've always been temporary. When you think of home, you think of a warm house with the porch light left on for you to arrive to. You don't think of a shitty motel with cockroaches in the walls and stains on the sheets. You don't think of me. I want to be a home for someone.

Healing

THE HORNETS IN MY STOMACH

You are here for a reason.
Whether you believe in a God,
who created you in magic dust
that flicked up in the air with a
twist of his fingers, you are here.
If you believe in the universe,
which took millions upon billions
of years to create atoms smashing
and stars colliding to make up
everything you know, you are here.
Or if you believe in something else,
you are here to smell flowers and
drink pink lemonade on hot summer
days and kiss many lips and swim
in the ocean and dance in the rain
and make friends and have a family
and look at the sky from which you
came from long ago, you are here.
All those long, late nights where you
could not sleep, all those drowsy
mornings where you didn't want to
get out of bed, all those times you've
cried so much your eyes dried out,
all that doesn't matter because you,
you perfect human being created out
of magic, you are here for a reason.

How to Love Yourself

Explore your body, for it is of the land. Whether it is big with rolling hills of tummy, or if it is tiny with valleys that climb into your ribs, it is important to map out every inch of it, so that you can fully understand who you are.

Know that you skin is but a canvas that you, the artist, have made art on. You may have scars, stretch marks, pimples, freckles, or even moles. All of these are strokes of paint that prove you have lived a wonderful life.

Look into the mirror every morning and repeat, "I am beautiful," until your tongue is numb. Your lips will get used to forming the words, and soon, your mind will start to believe it, and your eyes will start to see it.

Realize that, even if he no longer loves you, you are still worthy of being loved. You were beautiful before he loved you, and you are still beautiful after his love has faded away. You don't need him to be beautiful.

Learn to make yourself happy. Kiss your wounds, treat yourself right, stop yelling at yourself, don't put yourself down, and most importantly, take time for you and focus on your happiness. You deserve it.

How to Calm an Anxiety Attack

1. Inhale for 6 seconds.
Your breath might feel like it wants to escape
your lungs like a bird trying to break free
from a gilded cage, but try your hardest to
keep the air safely within your chest.

2. Hold your breath for 7 seconds.
My mother used to tell me to hold my breath
while driving past a cemetery. She said it was
to stop bad spirits from entering your body.
I don't believe in this anymore, but maybe
holding your breath stops the negative
thoughts from coming into your mind.

3. Exhale for 8 seconds.
You are the only one who can save yourself.
You are the only one who can take these breaths
and to keep yourself alive. People romanticize
a boy kissing your scars or a friend holding you
until you stop crying. But nobody gives you the
credit for picking up your own pieces when
nobody is there for you. It takes a strong and
powerful person to heal by themselves.

4. Repeat until you feel calm.
As you exhale, release your breath, but also
the bad thoughts that are causing your anxiety.
As you inhale, take in air, but also take in
positive thoughts to help you relax and heal.
Exhale: "I am worthless." "I can't do this."
Inhale: "I am doing my best." "I am ethereal."

He calls me his daisy, his rose,
his sweet little sunflower.
I may be a woman, and I may
be beautiful, but I am not weak.

I am poison ivy. I poison every
man who touches me with the
intent of ripping me out by my
roots. Do not touch me.

I am a Venus Flytrap. I ensnare
men who are foolish enough to
take advantage of me. You will
not come out alive.

I am a naked lady flower. My
pink petals cause cardiovascular
collapse. I break hearts in the
most painful way possible.

I am a Hemlock plant. The ancient
Greeks used me for execution. I
cause respiratory failure. Kiss me
and I'll take your breath away.

Don't make me your lily or daisy.
Women are not your pretty flowers
to rip petals out of. We are poisonous,
stinging with thorns, raging with grace.

THE HORNETS IN MY STOMACH

Call Me by My Name, or Nothing Else

He calls you anything but your name:
"Babe." "Gorgeous." "Hottie." "Cutie."
"Dollface." "Beautiful." "Sweetheart."
He calls you anything but your name,
as if you don't deserve a name at all.
You could be anybody, with any name,
but to him, you're "Sexy." It's a stand-in
for your real name. You're just a piece of
meat to him, and butchers never name
their cows before they slaughter them.
You know he's got a bunch of other girls,
and he can't remember their names either.
He uses these stick-on names to replace
the real names of these girls, and you're
one of them. But you're more than that.
You deserve to be called by your name,
and you deserve to be respected.

How to Love a Girl with Depression

1. Treat her gently. Her heart is made of a thousand pieces of broken glass and so is her skin. Loving her is like walking on eggshells. Be careful where you step, be careful where you touch. She may be close to breaking, so hold her tightly with your arms. Sometimes, you may be the only thing to keep her together.

2. Speak to her kindly. Your words are the rain under which she grows. She's heard so many words that beat her down, so use words to build her up. Call her on the phone. Hold her hand. Look her in the eyes. Tell her she looks beautiful. Tell her that her smile shines brighter than the sun. Tell her that she means more to the world than she knows.

3. Love her wholly. Depression empties the soul straight out of her. Her body may seem like an empty shell, but I promise that her heart is not as vacant. She loves you entirely, so she needs a love just as complete to fill the empty cracks in her skin. She keeps everyone out, but she trusts you enough to let you fill up her hollow ribcage.

4. Always come back. She will want to protect herself or to protect you from her. Maybe she doesn't want you to hurt her, so she will run away. Maybe she doesn't want to hurt you, so she will push you away. Know that she will be forever grateful that you are beside her. She is lost, so always, always find her.

THE HORNETS IN MY STOMACH

I think depression is so different than what people portray it as in the movies. Real life depression isn't any better or worse, but it's far less glamorized. My depression isn't overdosing on pills and waking up in a hospital with loved ones looking down over me. It's feeling dead inside and getting through the day with a fake smile painted on my face, and laughing at jokes that are no longer funny. It's continuing to live even though I do not want to because the pain of being so sad all the time is unbearable.

My depression isn't walking to a bridge in the early hours of the morning, where the sun hasn't risen yet and the mist covers my tears as I prepare to jump off. That's too picturesque. My depression is running outside my house at 2am to go lay down on the train tracks, only to give up halfway there and return back to my empty bed.

My depression isn't looking pretty while crying, as I dab at my eyes with my fingertips to not mess up my makeup. My depression is ugly crying. It's the absolutely hideous crying where you can't breathe and snot is running down your face along with tears and the rest of your mascara. My depression is the ugly crying where you tear out your hair and clench at your chest to keep your heart from falling out.

My depression isn't a short conversation with my parents, who learn about my depression and embrace me with a smile on their faces, knowing that I'll be okay. My depression is a long midnight talk with my mother and both of us are sobbing. She's crying because she thinks I'm going to kill myself. I'm crying because my sadness is not only hurting me, but it's hurting her as well.

My depression isn't just a road bump in my relationship with my boyfriend. In the movies, he'd be strong and supporting and I would cry in his arms and we would kiss in the rain until my tears stopped. My depression is me pushing him away and getting angry and wanting to be alone. My depression is being emotional and crying so much around him when all I want to do is be happy for him.

Don't let movies tell you how your depression should be. Depression isn't just a quirky trait to have to move the storyline along. It's a demon that wants to end the story altogether. Depression isn't pretty. Depression is really, really ugly. Don't feel bad by comparing your sadness to the fake sadness of a beautiful woman on TV. Don't feel as though your depression matters less because it isn't picturesque. Real life depression isn't scripted. You never know when you will break down. But that only makes you even stronger for handling its ugly unpredictability.

Men think they own a woman when they see her naked, when they have sex with her, when they touch between her thighs.
They don't understand that you cannot own someone based on where your fingers touch or where your eyes got to see.
You cannot own a woman whose very existence is not something to be owned. Women are forests to get lost in, oceans to drown in, cities to explore in. A mere man cannot tame something that is not to be tamed. Even if he gives her a ring, a woman is not a possession.
Men try to control things that they cannot understand.
Women are no exception, but that does not mean she lives to be shackled. Women are wild and passionate and free.

THE HORNETS IN MY STOMACH

Don't cling to a mistake just because you made love to it
and let it have its way with you past your clenched teeth.
Don't cling to a mistake just because it kissed you after it
hurt you, and you know it's not love, but it's close enough.
Don't cling to a mistake just because you thought it loved
you, and you denied the truth since you wanted forever.
Don't cling to a mistake just because it made promises to
you that it would stay, only to leave you without a trace.
Don't cling to a mistake just because you let it have a
big part of you, and now it won't give it back.
Don't cling to a mistake just because it had dark hair
and sharp eyes and looked so beautiful on top of you.
Don't cling to a mistake just because it took advantage
of you and made you do things you normally wouldn't.
Don't cling to a mistake just because it turned you into
a completely person than who you were before.
Don't cling to a mistake just because your regret won't
leave you alone or let you live life past that mistake.

I'm sick of a world where
boys think what makes a girl beautiful on the inside
is what's in between her legs,
and I'm sick of a world where
girls fall for bad boys who treat them like shit
and that's still the best they've ever been treated before,
and I'm sick of a world
that has sex crazed boys who care more about a girl's
bra size than the size of her heart,
as if 34D is going to offer more love than a smaller breast size,
and I'm sick of a world
where bottles clinking against teeth
and cigarettes burning our tongues
is considered the norm
and I'm sick of a world
where love is foreign
and lust is the most spoken language.

THE HORNETS IN MY STOMACH

A woman's body is not a treasure to steal.
You do not dig through her chest to find a
heart of gold to take away from her. You do
not X the spot between her legs for you to
plunder inside. You do not treat her like an
object for you to take for yourself and sail away.

A woman's body is not a pile of porno magazines.
She is not a page to spread open because her
value is beyond the spread of her legs. She is
more than sticky dog-eared pages stuck together
for you to glance at when you feel horny. She
is not a centerfold.

A woman's body is not a punching bag.
Do not hurl hurtful words and hard fists
at her. She is not there for you to beat up.
A woman is not to be degraded to a sand
bag that you use to take your frustrations
out on and throw away after.

A woman's body is not a graveyard.
She does not exist for you to hide the
skeletons of your closet within her. Do
not bury your mistakes and regrets in her
chest. She deserves more than the rotten
corpses that you dump in her.

Let's talk about regret. Let's talk about the boys you let touch you. Let's talk about how remembering his fingers inside you makes you want to vomit. Let's talk about how you didn't know that he was bad until it was too late. Let's talk about how he didn't reveal himself until after you slept with him. He shrugged his shoulders and shed his skin like a snake to reveal his inner evil. He slithered his fingers around your chin and sunk his fangs into your neck. You didn't realize until you fell for him, but his venom had already spread within you. Let's talk about how he acted nice until you let him have his way with you. Let's talk about the disgust you still feel after being taken advantage of.

But let's talk about revenge. The only way to kill a snake is by chopping off its head. He may have been a snake, but you are the one who holds the knife. You are the one who has legs and can walk away and move on with your life. Women have always been tricked by snakes. Even Eve befell at a serpent's charm. But once you get bitten, you know to cut off the head before the fangs get the chance to reach your throat. You may have let a snake poison you once, but you never will again.

THE HORNETS IN MY STOMACH

You learned to be scared of boys from a very young age.

In elementary school, you were taught that when a boy likes you, he will tease you. You were taunted every day. You had your hair pulled and got chased by boys who wanted to put a worm down your shirt. It was the day you got punched in the gut by one of them that your fear of boys really started.

In middle school, boys started getting worse. They became sexual, and boundaries started getting crossed. You were harassed on the bus by boys who humped the seat you sat on, and who poked your butt as you walked down the center aisle. They threw quarters at the back of your head in class, and you started to avoid them at all costs. You did not understand how other girls had crushes on these boys.

In high school, boys became monsters. You'd walk in the halls as boys smacked your butt, but you didn't give a response anymore because that's what they wanted. They'd make crude comments like, "Sit on my face, baby," and, "My parents aren't home. Do you want to come over and fuck?" You kissed two boys, and both of them shoved their hands down your jeans. You barely knew them.

In college, you go online and discover that many girls have been through this. Many have been raped by these boys. You don't understand what gives boys the right to own your body, but they've done it your whole life. You swear to yourself that you will never let another boy own your body again. You have the right to be respected. You have the right to be treated like a human being.

What People Don't Talk About Regarding Rape

People never talk about the healing process after sexual assault. They never talk about how it is to feel such extreme guilt and disgust at yourself. They never say how it feels to never be able to get his touch out from underneath your skin. They don't talk about the countless hour-long showers you take, crying and trying to scrub his touch from your flesh. They never talk about how to forgive yourself because you never said "yes," but you never said "no" either. They don't talk about the mixed emotions and the confusion. They don't talk about the dissociation. They don't talk about the repression of things that happened that make you forget mostly everything. They don't talk about how sex may be difficult now. They don't talk about the flashbacks you may get during sex that cause you to panic and cry. They don't talk about the self-hatred and the guilt you feel for letting it happen. And god, they do not talk about the pain. They never say how much it hurts. They never talk about how you have to live with it for the rest of your life. They tell you that you need to heal and forgive yourself, but they never tell you how.

THE HORNETS IN MY STOMACH

Headlines read:
UNCONSCIOUS WOMAN RAPED BEHIND DUMPSTER
and it seems to be the only kind of rape you ever hear about.
Rape is always done by a tall man in a dark alleyway. Rape is always committed by using a knife or a gun to coerce the woman into sex. Rape is always done to a woman who is drunk or unconscious. Rape is always a dramatic play reading that terrifies people reading headline stories. While rape is always a tragedy, it is not always so picturesque.

You never hear about women rapists. You never hear about men who are victims. You never hear about not saying "no," but definitely not saying "yes." You never hear about confusion or guilt or mixed emotions. You never hear about being raped in a safe place, like even your own bedroom. You never hear about friendly acquaintances who pressure you with no weapons but their hands up your shirt and their tongue down your throat. You never hear about rape being done while fully conscious, fully aware of what is happening, fully capable of feeling pain.

It makes you wonder if your rape really mattered. If it's not theatrical, does it really count as rape? Was it really rape if it wasn't behind a dumpster?

To the girl who never said no, but never really said yes:

1. He may have had his way with you. It might feel like he has burned down the forest that is your body. But forests always return. You may have been destroyed, but you will be okay. Give yourself time to regrow. You will come back as strong as ever, and next time, you will be strong enough to say no.

2. Your body is still a temple, even if he has tainted it. You should still treat your body as such. It is not a dumping ground for the dead bodies of your self-respect. It is not a punching bag where you hurl self-hate at. It is not a shitty motel where you let others come and go. It is a temple, even if it no longer feels like such. Your body, your temple, is utterly beautiful regardless of whom has set foot in it.

3. You may not have had the courage to say no, but that doesn't mean you are not allowed to say no ever again. Please remember that you are allowed to say no whenever you feel like it, even if you didn't say it before.

4. Your self-worth does not decrease by your silence. Your inability to say no does not make you a slut or a whore or cheap or trash. It does not make you worthless. You are of starlight, and just because you were temporarily touched by dark hands, that does not dim your incandescent shine.

Home

THE HORNETS IN MY STOMACH

The Welcome Mat on Your Lips

I've never had a home until
I found myself in your arms.
All my life, I've been lost.
I've roamed from empty rib
cage to empty rib cage, trying
to find somewhere warm for
my head to rest, but now I
have a home in your heart.

I want you, everywhere –
your lips between mine,
your fingers between mine.
You make me feel so whole
when everyone else left me
empty and hollow.

I need you, everywhere –
your waist between my legs,
your heart between my ribs.
You fill up all my
s p a c e s
so perfectly, my love.

THE HORNETS IN MY STOMACH

Love for us is not a horizon.
There is no distinct line where
sea ends and sky begins.
You kiss me so deeply that
I forget if I'm breathing in
your air or mine. We tangle
together and I lose track of
whose limbs are whose.
My skin blends into your
skin, and where my heart is,
yours is, too. We make love
and there is no longer a
distinction of where
you end and I begin.

I am so in love with you. I love you so much that the word "love" does not even begin to describe how I feel. The amount of feelings I have for you cannot be contained in a simple four letter word. I look at you and it's like seeing the sun after being in darkness my entire life up until now. You are the breath of air I take after being underwater for too long. You are the feeling of warmth by a fireplace after being in a blizzard for days on end. You are what I've been needing for so long, but never knew until I met you. The fact that you love me back just the same is such a miracle. It's hard to believe that someone as perfect as you could love someone like me, but you do.

THE HORNETS IN MY STOMACH

The Difference Between Him and You

He chased me into the bedroom, like the wolf chases a lamb, and devoured me slowly, painfully. His teeth were fangs and his hands were claws. Excitement became fear. Fear became death. Once he had his fill, he left. He walked out of the dark room and left me bleeding and torn apart on his bedsheets.

Your hands are gentle, and your heart is even gentler. Your fingers touch me as not to break me, and your kisses feel so soft upon my fragile skin. You treat me like gold, like I am the most precious thing you have ever held in your hands. You want to please me, but you want to love me even more.

What I said to you:
I love you.

What I wanted to say to you:
You are the very reason I wake up in the morning.
You are why the sun decides to rise each day,
and you are why the stars shine so brightly at night.
You are my world,
you are my everything.
Without you, I'd be nothing.
If only you knew how much love for you filled my heart.
I wish I could express my feelings for you with more than
I love you,
I love you,
I love you.

I Never Believed in Angels Until I Fell in Love with One

I am in love with an angel
who does not know he's an
angel. He does not notice
the golden halo glowing on
his head or the feathered
wings that fold over on his
shoulders. He does not know
that he fell from heaven into
my arms. He tells me that
the closest thing to heaven
that he knows of is waking
up beside me in bed each
morning. He finds rapture
in my lips and eternity in
my thighs. His skin feels
like the soft, weightless
clouds of which he came
from, and I hear the echoes
of god's harps in his voice.
How can one be so heavenly
but so unaware of it? How
can he not see that he was
touched by God's hands
himself? How does he not
know that God must have
sent him here to love me?

The boy I love doesn't know how to unhook my bra.

I thought I loved a boy once who unhooked my bra behind my back with one hand. He was too good at these kinds of things, and his hands were very skilled in ways that made me afraid. I knew by the way he kissed me that I wasn't the only person that his lips touched. He taught me how to have sex without putting feelings into it. He taught me how to love without putting feelings into it either.

The boy I love now doesn't know how to unhook my bra.
His fingers fumble for a while, trying to figure out the mechanics of the clasp. We laugh and I take it off for him. I kiss him and know that I am the only one he is kissing. My bra is the only one he has ever tried to undo. He taught me how to make love passionately. He taught me how to trust and fall and love again.

THE HORNETS IN MY STOMACH

The Difference Between Hell and Home

He runs his hand
up your thigh and
you've never felt
this afraid in all
of your life.

He grazes his thumb
on your cheek and
you've never felt
this calm in all
of your life.

A Haiku for Every Person I've Had Sex With:

You were my first and
I let you in because I
used to trust you then.

You touched me with your
filthy fingers and I hate
myself for that night.

It was a false love
but I was your first and I
think I broke your heart.

You were the first one
to teach me what it is like
to "make love," not "fuck."

THE HORNETS IN MY STOMACH

I've held an ocean in my arms.
His kisses filled my lungs with salt
water and he became something much
more than I was capable of. I was
overwhelmed by his waters and I
drowned before I learned to swim away.

I've held a wolf in my arms.
His howls echoed in my bones and
became my cries at night. He tore
my heart in half with his claws, and
it was then that I learned to never
open my heart to something so wild.

I've held a forest in my arms.
His vines and roots became entangled
in my skin and I could not get him
out of me. To be free, I set both of us
aflame. I caused a wildfire, but I
burned myself in the process.

I now hold you in my arms.
You are a universe, and your stars
reflected in your eyes. You are everything
I've ever known and everything I will
ever come to know. Never have I loved
anything that was so immensely beautiful.

Two Different Kinds of Sex:

I fucked a boy one night
and while he was inside me,
he asked me if it felt good.
I didn't know what to say.
It felt like I wasn't there,
probably because I didn't
want to be there under him.
I didn't know his middle name
or what he thinks about at night
when he can't sleep, or if he
even loved me [he didn't].

I made love to a boy this morning
and while he was inside me,
he asked me if it felt good.
I told him it was like liquid gold
melting every part of me.
It felt like fire was warming
each inch of my body.
Maybe it was because I knew
his middle name, and what he
thinks about when he can't sleep,
and if he loves me [he does].

THE HORNETS IN MY STOMACH

10 Reasons Why You Should Let Me Love You

1. I will cherish you like the gold you are.
You may think you are dirt to be stepped
on, but you are worth so much more.

2. You are the greatest masterpiece I've seen.
I will turn you into art. Even if you don't
think you are beautiful, I think you are.

3. I've learned to never pick the flowers that I find
most beautiful, or else they die. I water them
and let them bloom. I'll do the same with you.

4. I am the lighthouse amidst the raging sea. You
will sail through life and get lost along the way,
but I will always be here to guide you home.

5. Wildfires can destroy a whole forest, but after the last
ember dies, the forest revives and grows back stronger.
I will help you regrow after a wildfire ravages you.

6. You've loved people who have torn you apart.
But I will be the one to piece you back together,
even if the fragments of your skin cut my fingers.

7. You've fucked before, but that's not real.
I will show you what it's like to make love.
You will come to know what real love feels like.

8. When we kiss, I feel thunderstorms in my heart.
I feel static running through my veins. There is
electricity between us. I know you feel it, too.

9. I will hold onto you for a lifetime. I will never
let go of your hand because I am afraid of losing
you. I will never drop you, please don't be afraid.

10. I trust you with anything. You could put a loaded
gun in my mouth and I'd trust you to not pull the
trigger. I give you my life.

Ways to Say, "I Love You," Without Saying Those Three Words:

1. Please drive safely. I think that if you got into a car crash, my heart would be more damaged than your wrecked car. I need you to come home again.

2. I don't know what I'd do if you left me. I don't think that I could live anymore. It would feel like you plunged your hand into my chest and ripped out my heart. Please don't go.

3. When I hold you, I never want to let go. I feel like if I let you slip from my grasp, I might never get to hold you again. I guess that's why I always hold you so tightly.

4. The first time I kissed you felt like the last time I kissed you. I felt flowers bloom inside my ribcage and thunder resonate in my veins and oceans move inside my lungs. You amaze me.

5. You've asked me before, if I could live forever, would I? I've always said no, because I'm too sad to live. But now, I think otherwise. I'd live an eternity if you lived it with me.

THE HORNETS IN MY STOMACH

We kiss and our lips
scrape against each other
like rusty metal,
and yellow sparks
fly off our metallic teeth.
Our worn-out hips
grind against one another;
we fit together like
rotating gears.
The old, dusty lightbulbs
of our hearts flicker,
then start to glow
brightly again.
This is the first time
in years that either
of us have loved.
We fumble awkwardly,
not used to having
our fingers fit perfectly
in between someone else's.
We lost love, and
became robotic.
Love will turn us human.

You know
he loves you
when you wear
a baggy shirt
and he
kisses you
just the same
as when you are
wearing nothing
at all.

THE HORNETS IN MY STOMACH

I hate hickeys, but I like them
more when they are from you.
When you're gone, it reminds
me of that moment when your
lips were on my skin and your
hands were on my hips and you
were less than an inch away
from me. In a way. you are still
with me even though you are
gone. Your lips left, but your
kiss is still on my skin.

I've loved you for so long that you've become habit.
I cannot imagine falling in love with someone new.
It would be so very uncomfortable.
It'd be like trying on a new pair of shoes that are
too tight on your feet and don't allow your toes
room to move.
It'd be like moving away into a new house
that is nice, but will never feel like home.
It'd be like reading a new novel, and while it is
interesting, it isn't as good as your favorite book.
You are all I know. I don't want to learn someone else.
I don't want to learn the way their mouth curls up in a
smile, or how their hair looks out of the shower, or
what their laugh sounds like, or any of that.
I want to be with you and retrace the curves of
your back for the millionth time, and kiss your lips
like I always have [and hopefully, always will].
I want to come to know the wrinkles that
gradually settle on your face.
You are all I know, and you are all I ever want to know.

THE HORNETS IN MY STOMACH

Out of all
the paths
you could
have taken
in life, I'm
glad that
the one
you're on
led you
to me.

You know he's the one when
after everything goes wrong,
he looks you in the eyes,
and instead of saying,
"I can't do this anymore,"
he says, "I love you."

THE HORNETS IN MY STOMACH

I look into your eyes and it's like I'm looking at my home with the porch light left on for me at the front door. Your warm smile is the gently lit windows of somewhere I belong. You wrap me in your arms and it feels like home. I kiss you and I know that I belong nowhere else but with you.

Made in the USA
San Bernardino, CA
28 October 2017